# CONTENTS

# A Quick Note

*Special thanks to my wife Sharon for always believing in me and my crazy ideas, and a big shout out to my family and friends who tested every one of these questions (and the hundreds of others that didn't make the cut).*

The world is not a boring place, but we find ourselves bored so often because we haven't been asking the right questions. You are holding 300 questions that have already sparked thousands of conversations that have helped strangers begin to bond as friends, friends grow closers, and spouses discover new things about one another after years of marriage. If you've ever felt bored in a conversation at some boat anchor of a party, an interesting question can change not only your outlook on the party but the party itself.

## Recommendation

Over the last few months Joe has put together a string of daily questions. I have taken those questions and used them with family, friends, and clients. Some create great and deep dialog about things in the past, some create funny moments that bring fun insight to others, and some just are fun to work through during a conversation. I cannot recommend this book strongly enough. Use it, and have fun!

- Richard A. Branham
*Author, What Are The Odds?*

# HYPOTHETICALLY

*Questions 1-32*

1. You are going to spend 5 minutes of every day for the next year doing something you currently don't do. What do you choose?

2. You are forced to take a cold weather vacation. Where do you go?

3. You are gifted enough money to build a vacation home anywhere you want, but it becomes the only place you can vacation from now on. Where do you build it?

4. You have unlimited money for a 24 hour vacation. Where do you go, and what do you do?

5. If you and you alone had to cook something from scratch for the Queen tonight, what would you make?

6. If you could be a master at any cooking technique, which would you choose?

7. If you had to spend a day watching the same movie over and over again, which movie would you choose?

8. You can spend a 2 week vacation in any movie universe. Which do you visit?

9. Where would you go if you were going to take a 2 hour vacation?

10. If you could be the best in the world at any skill, what would you choose?

11. Tomorrow you will wake up fluent in a new language. Which do you choose?

12. If time and money were no object for your supper tonight, what would you be eating?

13. If you had to eat at the same restaurant every day for a month, which would you choose?

14. Where would you go if you had to take a week long vacation alone and if you couldn't visit anyone you know?

15. If you could win the gold medal in any Olympic event, which would you want to win?

16. You're on a road trip and you stop for lunch.

What kind of place did you have your meal?

17. You're on a road trip and the only place to get anything for lunch is a gas station. What do you buy?

18. It's 8:30 in the evening, and you're looking for a snack. What do you eat?

19. If time stopped and froze everyone except you for an hour every day, what would you do with your hour?

20. Your next vacation will be exhaustively exploring a city you haven't been to yet. Which city do you choose?

21. You are opening a coffee shop, and to bring in new customers, you are given the ability to have an exclusive acoustic concert from any artist. Which artist would you choose?

22. You are opening a restaurant where you are guaranteed to have the world greatest version of any dish you choose. What would your specialty be?

23. You are given $1 billion for a completely frivolous upgrade to your home. You can do anything, but it must not solve a real problem. What do you do?

24. If you could be teleported to any restaurant you've never been to and immediately served a free meal, which restaurant would you choose?

25. You can have your great great grandchildren watch one TV series to know what your family growing up was like. What do you have them watch?

26. You are hired by an incredibly prestigious university to teach one class. What do you teach?

27. You are given a free vacation, but you can only use one adjective to describe the kind of vacation you'd like to take to the travel agent. What word do you say?

28. If you could be guaranteed to win any real-life award if you worked for it, which award would you choose?

29. You are given a pet monkey. What is his or her name?

30. What career do you think you have in an alternate universe?

31. You are going to go on a non-religious pilgrimage. Where do you go?

32. You are given a year to research any topic as your

full-time job. What specifically do you research?

# ALL OVER THE PLACE

*Questions 33-70*

33. You are going to spend a year abroad with no technological connectivity. Where do you go?

34. You are going to spend 1 hour anywhere in the world you want, but after that hour you can never go there again. Where do you choose?

35. What was your favorite road trip?

36. When you travel what is important to you?

37. What US city have you never been to but would really like to go?

38. What is your must-have road trip snack?

39. What is the best place you've never been?

40. Where is your home away from home?

41. What tourist attraction is worth the hassle?

42. What popular vacation destination has no interest for you?

43. Aside from location, what is your secret to a great vacation?

44. Where would you go on a road trip if you had to turn around as soon as you reached your destination?

45. Where have you been that made history come alive?

46. Where is the place that is kindred to the essence of who you are?

47. Where is the farthest you have been from civilization?

48. Where is the most inspiring place you've been?

49. What is the first thing you think about when planning a vacation?

50. When did you first fall in love with the place you love the most?

51. Where are you most yourself?

52. What was the best unexpected occurrence on one of your vacations?

53. Where is the most other-worldly place you've been?

54. How has your dream vacation changed over the years?

55. Where are you looking forward to going to visit someday?

56. What restaurant that you've visited on vacation do you wish you could visit today?

57. What local tourist attraction is worth visiting?

58. What place surprised you by how wonderful it was to be there?

59. What are the essential elements of an incredible stay-cation?

60. Where did you go on your first grownup vacation?

61. Where is the most unexpected place you have found yourself?

62. What is your favorite keepsake from a vacation?

63. Which three adjectives best describes your three favorite places? Use one for each.

64. What unpopular place do you love to go to?

65. What place best shaped how you view yourself?

66. What was the most unique thing you've done on vacation?

67. What place are people surprised to hear that you've been there?

68. What tourist attraction have you never seen but would really like to go?

69. What country that you've never been to holds a special place in your heart?

70. What was happening when you realized your best vacation was happening?

# SCHOOL YEARS

*Questions 71-117*

71. How was your drivers test?

72.  Why was your favorite teacher in high school your favorite?

73. What was your best moment in high school?

74. Where was the greatest non-theme-park place to go when you were a kid?

75. What was your childhood obsession?

76. What were you sure of as a teenager that you aren't sure of anymore?

77. Where was your favorite hang out spot when you were a teenager?

78. What was your dream job when you were 16?

79. You can re-live one great evening from your

teenage years. What did you do that night?

80. What childhood toy do you wish you still had?

81. What hobby did you have as a teenager that you don't do anymore?

82. Who was your favorite celebrity when you were 13?

83. What did you do as a pre-teen that you wish you still did?

84. What 3 movies would you watch if 14 year old you was having a slumber party tonight?

85. What high school class do you wish you could take again?

86. What gave you the greatest sense of joy when you were in 2nd grade?

87. Who were the 3 most influential non-family members in your life at age 16?

88. What was your go-to leisure activity when you were in middle school?

89. What did you do as a teenager to try to feel more mature?

90. Where did your money go when you were a teenager?

91. What were the 3 most important things to you in middle school?

92. What was the highlight of your summers when you were an elementary student?

93. What school project do you still remember fondly?

94. What was your go-to after school snack in elementary school?

95. What is your best first day of school memory?

96. What TV character from your childhood did you relate to most?

97. What made you feel special when you were young?

98. What did you parents do especially well for you?

99. What was your most prized possession when you were a child?

100. What grade level in school was the most impactful for you?

101. What do you remember about your parents' driving habits?

102. What do you remember being your first favorite meal?

103. What did you do to occupy your time as a child that you still love to do today?

104. What candy would you go crazy for when you were a kid?

105. What are you thankful to have left behind in your teenage years?

106. What was your favorite way to spend recess?

107. What was your biggest purchase before you were 16?

108. What was your favorite thing about the home you grew up in?

109. What was your favorite dream from your childhood?

110. What school lunch made you absurdly happy?

111. Where did you want to live when you were a teenager?

112. What was your greatest accomplishment as a teenager?

113. What was your favorite pair of shoes when you were a kid?

114. What did you collect when you were a kid?

115. What was your favorite thing to do outside when you were a kid?

116. Who was the first movie star in your world world when you were a kid?

117. What did you pretend to like when you were a kid so you could fit in?

# MOVIES, MUSIC, SHOWS

## Questions 118-161

118. What movie do you wish everyone liked a little more?

119. What is the best movie in the genre you like the least?

120. You will only be listening to 2 albums for the rest of your days. Which albums?

121. How has a movie changed your life?

122. What is your favorite song from a movie or musical?

123. What was the first movie you remember seeing in a theater?

124. What movie best sums up the previous year of

your life?

125. What is your go-to romantic comedy?

126. What movie score makes your heart soar?

127. What movie was cast flawlessly?

128. What movie teaches the most profound life lessons?

129. Who is the best music artist in the genre you like the least?

130. What is your favorite song that came out before you were born?

131. What movie best depicts your outlook on life?

132. Who is your favorite unpopular music artist?

133. What show do you love but it seems like most people haven't seen?

134. What is an unlikely movie that to moved you to tears?

135. What song always stirs up something good in you?

136. If your favorite music artist was an activity,

what would it be doing?

137. What song is currently in the heaviest rotation in your head?

138. What obscure song do you love?

139. What artist is the soundtrack of your favorite vacation spot?

140. What movie best describes your mood this week?

141. What was your favorite piece of media you consumed yesterday?

142. What TV show is your guilty pleasure?

143. What movie has the most nostalgia for you?

144. What song is pure magic for you these days?

145. What is your favorite movie to watch in the fall?

146. What TV show or movie do you think your personality would fit best in?

147. What song lyric or line of poetry makes your heart flutter with goodness?

148. What movie release were you the most excited about in your life?

149. What song was your jam in high school?

150. What is your favorite movie that was released before you were born?

151. Which cartoon is the best cartoon?

152. You're given the ability to see a movie for the very first time again. Which movie would you choose?

153. Who makes something and you immediately want to experience it?

154. What is your favorite movie from the decade you were born?

155. Who was your first favorite music artist?

156. You have 1 movie to describe your taste in movies. Which movie do you choose?

157. How did you discover your favorite music artist?

158. What song are you most likely to listen to on repeat?

159. Who comes to your mind most prominently when you think about Rock and Roll?

160. What show are you currently binge watching?

161. Which show's theme song do you love?

# FOOD

## Questions 162-206

162. What food are you craving right now?

163. What non-traditional movie theater snack should become traditional?

164. What side dish could you eat for a meal?

165. What is your favorite homemade preparation of potatoes?

166. If your personality were a meal, what would it be?

167. What is the best thing you can get from a specific fast food restaurant?

168. What genre of music best describes your favorite restaurant?

169. In great detail, describe your ideal burger.

170. Which bread with what topping makes the best toast?

171. What meal best symbolizes your teenage years?

172. What are the ingredients to a perfect summer picnic?

173. In great detail, describe your perfect breakfast.

174. Apart from taste, what food is the most experientially fun to eat?

175. What is the most refreshing summer beverage, and under what circumstances is it best consumed?

176. What meal is delicious, but you only handle it once in awhile?

177. What always tastes better homemade than it does at a restaurant?

178. What food combination would people love more if they were you?

179. What appetizer makes your mouth water just thinking about it?

180. What messy meal is worth the clean up afterwards?

181. What sandwich makes you wonder why you ever eat anything else?

182. What food were you hesitant about trying but now love?

183. What was the last thing you ate that was truly scrumptious?

184. Which pizza is the best pizza?

185. How do you make the perfect grilled cheese sandwich?

186. What snack is uniquely you?

187. What is the perfect snowy night comfort food?

188. What is food is delicious in adulthood but was disgusting in childhood?

189. What food do you wish you knew about earlier in life?

190. What is the most sophisticated meal in your cooking repertoire?

191. What no-so-good for you ingredient do you wish you could make a super-food?

192. What is your go-to party food?

193. What is you favorite low effort sweet treat to make?

194. What is the your favorite way to make chicken?

195. You just an entire bag of chips by yourself. What kind were they?

196. You are going to pig out at home. What's on the menu?

197. What meal in your cooking repertoire is the perfect intersection of delicious and healthy?

198. In great detail, describe your perfect chocolate dessert.

199. What food do you forget how good it is until you are eating it again?

200. Where is your favorite place to eat breakfast?

201. You are going to celebrate something big happening in your life with a stupendous meal. What are you having and where are you eating it?

202. What kind of cheese makes you melt into happiness?

203. Which fruit based dessert is the best fruit based dessert?

204. What is the most important ingredient to make a pizza spectacular for you?

205. What is the best thing you haven't eaten in more than a year?

206. What is the most recent thing you ate that gave you great joy?

# RANDOM QUESTIONS

*Questions 207-300*

207. Where is the place that you recommend everyone should go?

208. Which animated character do you relate to most?

209. Where did you go on your first date?

210. What board game are you passionate about?

211. What villain do you resonate with most?

212. What needs to happen for you to begin to feel the holiday spirit?

213. What little thing makes you way more happy than it should?

214. How much time off of work do you need to feel like you're on vacation?

215. Apart from your profession, what are you an expert in?

216. What activity were you surprised to love after trying it?

217. How are you and your dad alike?

218. What smell triggers happy memories for you?

219. Of the people you have never met, who has had the biggest influence in your life?

220. What soul filling thing is common in your life but is uncommon in the general populace?

221. What does relaxation taste like for you?

222. What was the first website you remember visiting?

223. What musical instrument best encompasses your personality?

224. What tastes like springtime?

225. What do you do when you want to feel fancy?

226. What has given you the greatest sense of accomplishment in the past year?

227. What purchase has given you the most bang for your buck?

228. What was the most important thing you learned at your first job?

229. What has been the biggest life goal you've achieved so far?

230. What specific restaurant location has the fondest memories for you?

231. What has been the biggest help in you discovering who you were made to be?

232. What was the best feature in your first car?

233. What is your favorite thing to spend money on?

234. What is the classiest thing you own?

235. What is your formula for productivity?

236. What are you almost too embarrassed to admit that you love?

237. Who would be surprised to learn just how

much they changed your life for the better?

238. What is your favorite topic to discuss at a high intellectual level?

239. What is your favorite mindless game to play?

240. What is your favorite thing about a culture that isn't your own?

241. What character trait do you think is your strongest?

242. What subject piques your curiosity today but it didn't interest you a year ago?

243. What event you attended was so good it was practically magical?

244. What has been the biggest win for you in the past month?

245. What outfit is quintessentially you?

246. What personal endeavor makes you feel most proud?

247. Where do you find yourself most spiritually alive?

248. What is the most important thing you learned

about yourself recently?

249. What quest are you on?

250. What do you most often think about when there is nothing pressing to think about?

251. What is your favorite way of taking care of yourself?

252. What brand has had the most positive influence in your life?

253. Why do you think you like your preferred source of entertainment so much?

254. What has been your favorite costume you've worn?

255. What is your most satisfying creative outlet?

256. What group or club helped you become a better you?

257. What is your favorite word that you or your family or friends made up?

258. What restaurant best encompasses your personality?

259. What is the best way your life has moved for-

ward recently?

260. What was happening the first time you remember feeling joy?

261. What is your favorite reason to get up to start your day way before you normally do?

262. What modern convenience do you feel like you're better off for not using it?

263. How did you discover what you love about yourself the most?

264. What brings your heart back to a grateful place?

265. What is the next milestone you are looking forward to passing in your life?

266. What has been your biggest affirmation recently?

267. What is your favorite memory with your first car?

268. What is an unexpected way you have been shown that you are loved?

269. What topic would you give a talk about if you had a room full of world leaders?

270. What was your first big decision?

271. What do you like to watch that isn't on a screen?

272. What happened at your best day of work?

273. What is your air travel story?

274. What word makes you excited?

275. What is your most quirky possession?

276. What was the cool thing to do in your high school when you were a student?

277. What is your town's best restaurant?

278. What is not an actual day-off-of-work holiday but really should be?

279. What is your favorite book to recommend?

280. What is something you really enjoyed learning about recently?

281. What would your 14 year old self be most happy to learn about your life today?

282. How are you still like a little kid?

283. What were you doing the last time you felt cultured?

284. What kids show did you enjoy when you were probably too old to be watching kids shows?

285. Where were you the last time you felt pure joy?

286. What is the most historically important thing you've traveled to see?

287. What was the first thing you remember learning to cook?

288. What is something you've changed your mind about?

289. What was the last thing that truly "wowed" you?

290. How has your life become better recently?

291. What restaurant do you love but not enough to make going there a priority?

292. What is the most comfortable thing you own?

293. What is your favorite part of your commute to work?

294. What was your first favorite book?

295. Where was the first place you remember driving to when you got your license?

296. What have you been doing for fun recently?

297. What was your first favorite show?

298. Why do you live where you live?

299. What is the oldest thing you own?

300. How did you learn to do the thing you love to do the most?

Made in the USA
Lexington, KY
11 March 2019